Parkland school shooting

Why the gunman was spared the death penalty

By

Paul J. Ward

TABLE OF CONTENTS

<u>Parkland school shooting overview</u>

At Marjory Stoneman Douglas High School in Parkland, Florida, a Miami suburb, 19-year-old Nikolas Cruz opened fire on students and staff on February 14, 2018, killing 17 people and wounding 17.

Former student Cruz, who escaped the scene on foot by appearing to be one of the other pupils, was apprehended without incident about an hour later in Coral Springs, close by.

"A pattern of disciplinary concerns and unsettling behavior" was looked at by the police and the prosecution.

The shooting spree surpassed the Columbine High School tragedy in Colorado in April 1999, which resulted in 15 fatalities, including the perpetrators, becoming the bloodiest high school shooting in American history.

After the tragic shootings in Paradise, Nevada, and Sutherland Springs, Texas, in October and November 2017, there was a spike in public support for gun control.

The organization "Never Again MSD," which campaigns for gun reform, was created by Parkland students.

On March 9, Governor Rick Scott signed a bill that further restricted Florida's gun laws and authorized the arming of teachers who had completed the necessary training as well as the hiring of school resource officers.

The Broward County Sheriff's Office received criticism for how it handled the police response, both for choosing to wait outside the school rather than dealing with Cruz immediately away and for ignoring many warnings about him despite a long history of threatening behavior.

Several police officers who attended the scene resigned as a result, and Sheriff Scott Israel was fired. A commission set up by then-Governor Scott to look into the massacre denounced the police's passivity and demanded that school districts all around the state adopt stronger security measures.

On October 20, 2021, Cruz pleaded guilty to all charges and expressed regret for his actions. In January 2022, a four-month trial with the death sentence on the table was scheduled to begin. The COVID-19 pandemic contributed to several delays in the sentencing phase.

Cruz's death penalty trial lasted from July 18, 2022, through October 13, 2022, when the jury recommended Cruz be given a life sentence without the possibility of parole.

The incident

Approximately 45 miles (72 km) northwest of Miami and 30 miles (48 km) northwest of Fort Lauderdale, in the affluent community of Parkland, Florida, the shooting took place on February 14, 2018, in the late afternoon at Marjory Stoneman Douglas High School.

Nikolas Cruz, the shooter, was seen by cops carrying a bag and a weapon case. He was spotted by a staff member, who noticed him and radioed a colleague to say that he was heading "purposefully" in the direction of Building 12. He did not, however, pursue the shooter or issue a "Code Red" to secure the school. Later, the first employee stated that his training only instructed him to report threats, while his coworker hid in a closet.

Cruz walked into Building 12, a three-story structure with 30 classrooms that typically housed 900 students and 30 teachers. Cruz started arbitrarily shooting at students and teachers as soon as he entered a hallway while toting an AR-15-style semi-automatic rifle and numerous magazines.

The fire alarm may have been activated by Cruz or by the smoke from the gunfire, but whichever way it happened, it puzzled everyone because there had been a fire drill earlier in the day. Cruz started by shooting through the windows of four closed classroom doors, killing three kids in the hallway before continuing to shoot through the doors, killing six more students and injuring thirteen more.

Students were unable to take cover in many of the classrooms in Building 12 because of the lack of "hard corners," locations where people could securely hide if a gunman peeked through a window or door, and furniture frequently blocking potential safe areas.

Ivy Schamis was instructing a class on overcoming hatred when Cruz opened fire in her classroom, killing two of the pupils she was teaching. Five or six pupils from Schamis' class suffered injuries. Cruz may have scrawled swastikas on the ammunition magazines he left at the school, but according to Schamis, Cruz had no idea he was shooting into a Holocaust class.

Due to uncertainty among school staff over who had the power to do so, a "Code Red" was still not called as the shooting took place. After finding a victim's body and hearing the shooting, a staff member finally ordered a lockdown at around 2:21 pm.

When the shooting started, there was an armed school resource officer from the Broward County Sheriff's Office on campus. He stayed outside between Building 12 and the neighboring Building 7.

Cruz moved to the second level where he opened fire into two more classrooms without hitting anyone after killing two staff members next to a stairwell.

He shot and killed five pupils who were stuck in the hallway on the third level, along with another staff member, and injured four more. He then entered a teachers' lounge and made an unsuccessful attempt to shoot through the hurricane-resistant windows facing the yard to hit staff and pupils fleeing below.

Cruz stopped shooting (perhaps because his gun jammed) and dropped it on the third floor of the building before blending in with the escaping students to exit the scene. After getting a soda at a mall on the way, he continued walking to a fast food restaurant where he lingered until 3:01 p.m. before departing on foot.

Cruz was apprehended by police as the alleged gunman 2 miles (3.2 km) away from the school in Coral Springs' Wyndham Lakes area at around 3:40 p.m. Then, with "labored breathing," he was brought to a hospital emergency department. Cruz was taken back into police custody after 40 minutes and then placed in the Broward County Jail.

In just under four minutes, all of the victims were shot during the roughly six-minute massacre. Cruz was identified as the shooter on the school security camera footage and by witnesses.

Additional paramedics from the nearby Fire-Rescue department continuously asked to enter the facility while SWAT paramedics were already inside. Even after the defendant was taken into custody, the Broward Sheriff's Office rejected these requests.

There were seventeen fatalities and seventeen other wounded but alive victims. The day following the shooting, three people were still in critical condition, and one person was still there the next day.

<u>Fatalities</u>

Twelve victims passed away within the structure, three outside on school grounds, and two in hospitals.

The three employees as well as the fourteen pupils that died were:

Alyssa Alhadeff, 14

Scott Beigel, 35

Martin Duque, 14

Nicholas Dworet, 17

Aaron Feis, 37

Jaime Guttenberg, 14

Chris Hixon, 49

Luke Hoyer, 15

Cara Loughran, 14

Gina Montalto, 14

Joaquin Oliver, 17

Alaina Petty, 14

Meadow Pollack, 18

Helena Ramsay, 17

Alex Schachter, 14

Carmen Schentrup, 16

Peter Wang, 15

After opening a classroom door so that students might enter and flee from Cruz, geography teacher Scott Beigel was slain.

Security guard and assistant football coach Aaron Feis was slain while defending two pupils.

The school's athletic director, Chris Hixon, was shot and died as he hurried toward the sound of gunshots and attempted to assist children who were running away.

Student Peter Wang was last seen holding doors open for other students in his Junior Reserve Officers' Training Corps (JROTC) uniform. When Cruz arrived and opened fire, Wang was unable to flee with the other students. Commentators praised his deeds and dubbed him a hero. His burial with full military honors was demanded in a White House petition that went around.

Wang was buried in his JROTC Blues uniform, and the U.S. Army posthumously awarded the ROTC Medal for Heroism to him, Alaina Petty, and Martin Duque at their respective funerals. He received a coveted posthumous acceptance to the United States Military Academy on February 20.

For the Parkland Soccer Club, Alyssa Alhadeff served as captain. The United States women's national soccer team honored her before a match in Orlando on March 7, 2018, or just over three weeks after the shooting. In addition to receiving official jerseys with her name on them, her teammates and family were invited to the game.

Senior Meadow Pollack suffered four gunshot wounds. Pollack attempted to enter a classroom by crawling to the door as Cruz fired into other classes, but was unsuccessful. Freshman Cara Loughran was standing next to Pollack, and Pollack tried to protect Loughran from the gunfire by covering her.

After entering the classroom again, the gunman sought out Pollack and Loughran, where he killed both girls with five more shots from his rifle.

<u>Survivors and injuries</u>

Anthony Borges, a 15-year-old patient, was the final victim to be released from the hospital on April 4. Known as "the real Iron Man," Borges was shot five times after blocking the door of a classroom with 20 children using his own body as a shield.

After being freed, Borges released a statement in which he denounced the conduct of the Broward Sheriff's deputies, Sheriff Scott Israel, and School Superintendent Robert Runcie. To recoup costs associated with his treatment, his family has given notice of its intention to sue the school district for bodily injury.

The 2018 BET Awards presented Borges with a humanitarian award.

The victims of the massacre, including instructors and students, have grappled with survivor's guilt and other PTSD symptoms. After having difficulty attending college, Sydney Aiello, 19, who had survived the shooting and whose friend Meadow Pollack had been killed, committed suicide on March 17, 2019, thirteen months after the incident. She had been treated for PTSD and survivor's guilt in addition to her fear of being in a classroom. A 16-year-old boy who had survived the shooting committed suicide less than a week later.

The USC Shoah Foundation's first-ever Stronger Than Hate Educator Award was given to teacher Ivy Schamis in 2019.

Nicholas Dworet and Helena Ramsay, who lost their lives in her class as a result of the shooting, were remembered by Schamis during her acceptance speech during the ceremony.

The perpetrator

Nikolas Jacob Cruz, the perpetrator, was adopted by Lynda and Roger Cruz when he was just a baby. He was born in Margate, Florida, on September 24, 1998. Roger passed away on August 11, 2004, at the age of 67, and Lynda passed away on November 1, 2017, leaving him without a biological parent. Three months before the shooting, Cruz became an orphan.

Since the passing of his mother, he has been residing with family and friends. He was working at a nearby Dollar Tree and engaged in a GED program at the time of the shooting.

According to CNN, Cruz was a JROTC member who had won numerous honors, "including academic accomplishment for maintaining an A grade in JROTC and Bs in other areas." He also competed on the varsity air rifle squad at his school.

Social media use and behavioral difficulties of Cruz

According to The Washington Post, Cruz had behavioral issues since middle school and was "entrenched in the procedure for getting pupils to help rather than sending them to law enforcement."

Six times in three years, he changed schools to address these issues. He was moved in 2014 to a school for students with emotional or cognitive problems. There have been rumors that he threatened other students.

Two years later, he went back to Stoneman Douglas High School but was dismissed in 2017 for disciplinary issues.

As he could not be entirely dismissed from the Broward County School system, he was moved to an alternative setting. Cruz had threatened other pupils, the school administration had sent out an email to instructors informing them of this. He was not permitted to have a backpack on campus by the school.

Beginning in 2013, Cruz's involuntary admittance to a residential treatment center was advised by psychiatrists. In September 2016, the Florida Department of Children and Families looked into him after he posted on Snapchat that he had cut both of his arms and intended to get a pistol.

At this point, a school resource officer proposed that he submit to a Baker Act-mandated involuntary mental examination.

A psychiatric hospital disagreed, but two guidance counselors did. He was diagnosed with autism, ADHD, and depression, according to state investigators (ADHD). He was found to be "at minimal risk of injuring himself or others," according to their assessment. He had previously undergone mental health therapy, but in the year before the shooting, he had not.

Cruz's online personas and accounts were "extremely, very frightening," according to Broward County Sheriff Scott Israel.

They featured images and posts of him brandishing various weapons, such as shotguns, pistols, BB guns, and long knives. He was described by police as having "extreme" views, and social media profiles that were allegedly connected to him posted offensive language towards Muslims and people of color.

Links to his YouTube remarks include "I want to die. Threats against police officers, fighting (sic), killing (sic), and "Antifa" ", and a desire to resemble the shooting at the University of Texas tower. Cruz has a profile picture on Instagram of a person sporting a "Make America Great Again" baseball cap.

Cruz legally bought an AR-15-style semi-automatic rifle from a Coral Springs gun dealer in February 2017 after passing the necessary background checks. He had previously similarly acquired many additional weapons, including multiple rifles and at least one shotgun.

In Florida at the time of the shooting, purchasing firearms from federally authorized dealers was permissible for those as young as 18 years old. This included the rifle that was allegedly used in the shooting. Since then, the minimum age limit has been increased to 21.

Police found items at the scene, including pistol magazines with swastika symbols, cut into them.

Cruz allegedly wrote "I hate niggers" and a swastika on his backpack, according to one pupil. According to CNN, Cruz espoused racist, homophobic, antisemitic, and xenophobic opinions in a closed Instagram group chat. Cruz routinely talked about the firearms he owned and declared his hatred for "Jews, niggers, and immigrants." Cruz once declared in the group chat, "I think I am going to kill people," though he later insisted that he was joking.

Cruz allegedly had anger management difficulties and frequently made jokes about weapons and gun violence, including threats to blow up places of business, according to a former classmate.

He was "very stressed out all the time, talked about firearms a lot, and attempted to cover his face," according to the brother of a 2016 graduate. At the time of the incident, a student who was enrolled there stated, "I think everyone had in their minds that if anyone was going to do it, it was going to be him."

During his sophomore year, a classmate who was put in charge of helping him claimed, "He described to me how he was expelled from two private institutions.

Twice, he was restrained. He wanted to go into the military. He liked to go hunting." According to the mother of a student, he also boasted about butchering animals. According to a neighbor, his mother would summon the police to the house to try to get him to grow up.

Advance notices to law enforcement

Although this number is disputed, Sheriff Scott Israel claimed that his office got 23 calls regarding Cruz during the previous ten years. Using a public records request, CNN was able to get a sheriff's office call log, which revealed that between 2008 and 2017, at least 45 calls mentioning Cruz, his brother, or the family residence were made.

Cruz was the subject of anonymous tips on two occasions: on February 5, 2016, regarding a threat to shoot up the school; and on November 30, 2017, regarding Cruz's potential as a "school shooter in the making" and his propensity for amassing knives and firearms.

His attempted suicide and intention to purchase a gun were reported to the school resource officer on September 23, 2016, and the school said it would conduct a "threat assessment" as a result.

Cruz should be committed for a mental health evaluation, according to two counselors at the school and a sheriff's deputy who served as a resource officer at Stoneman Douglas.

"I'm going to be a professional school shooter," read the comment someone with the pseudonym "Nikolas Cruz" left on a YouTube video on September 24, 2017.

The comment was reported to the FBI by the person who posted the video on YouTube.

Agent Robert Lasky claims that despite database searches, the agency was unable to identify the person who made the threatening remark.

The FBI got a tip on its Public Access Line on January 5, 2018, less than two months before the shooting, from someone close to Cruz. The agency stated on February 16, two days after the shooting, that included this information.

The caller discussed Cruz's access to firearms, desire to murder people, unpredictable behavior, and frightening social media posts, as well as the possibility that he would carry out a massacre at a school, according to the statement. The FBI stated the tip line violated protocol when the material was not transmitted to the Miami Field Office, where investigative action would have been taken, after performing an investigation. The FBI started looking into how the tip line operated.

There has been criticism of Israel and other Broward County Sheriff's Office personnel for their silence in the face of several warning signs and red flags regarding Cruz.

Calls for Israel's resignation became louder in the days that followed the massacre as new details about the department's inaction came to light.

Israel declined to step down soon after the shooting, telling CNN in an interview that he had "provided outstanding leadership to this organization" while disclaiming accountability for the actions of his deputies. Israel was ultimately replaced as sheriff by Gregory Tony after all of this by Governor Ron DeSantis.

<u>Attempts to get assistance</u>

A review of Cruz's treatment was done by the school system. According to their redacted assessment, which was examined in August 2018 by The New York Times, The Daily Beast, and other media, Cruz had consulted education professionals a year before the massacre because his performance at Stoneman Douglas was deteriorating. Cruz at the age of eighteen visited the doctors' offices with his mother. He should transfer to Cross Creek School in Pompano Beach, where he had previously excelled, according to the professionals.

However, he rejected this choice since he wanted to graduate from Stoneman Douglas with his class and was of legal age.

He was informed that he would lose access to special education services if he stayed, but this was untrue.

He left a few months later as a result of poor grades. Cruz then asked to go to Cross Creek, but he was rejected and told a new examination was required, delaying action.

Why the shooter was not given the death penalty

Many families left the court in Florida on Thursday confused and in tears. It was the deadliest mass shooting to reach a jury trial in the United States.

Peter Wang's victim Lynn Chen's cousin remarked, "We are surprised by this result because it is so unjust." How is he able to endure another day?

Nikolas Cruz shot and killed 17 people at Marjory Stoneman Douglas High School in 2018, prompting the jury to recommend life in prison instead of the death penalty.

The decision caused an emotional outcry from the relatives of the victims who had gathered in the court.

Linda Schulman, a mother, remarked, "This animal is still going to serve life in prison without the possibility of parole. I pray he lives with fear in him always".

Ivy Schamis, a teacher in Parkland who testified during the trial about how two students in her class perished in the attack, told the BBC that she was heartbroken.
She said, "He [the shooter] will enjoy his life. It indicates that the majority of parents won't outlast this shooter since "he will get love letters." After this, I no longer have any faith in the legal system".

After the sentencing hearing, three of the jury's twelve members decided to spare the shooter.

According to Florida law, a unanimous vote is required for someone to be executed. The offender is given a life sentence without the possibility of parole if there is just one dissenting vote on the jury. This is the current situation the Parkland shooter, aged 24, is in.

Benjamin Thomas, the jury foreman, told CBS Miami that he "wasn't thrilled with how [the sentencing] panned out" and that he did not support the life term.

He stated, "It essentially came down to one particular juror who thought [the shooter] was mentally ill. She didn't think he should be executed because of his mental illness".

He said, "There was one [juror] who had a strong no; she couldn't do it. "And there were two more who ultimately cast their votes in the same manner."

The jury, which was made up of five women and seven men, did decide that there were sufficient aggravating circumstances to support the death penalty.

Following Florida's law, a death sentence may be imposed if 16 aggravating elements are present.

For instance, the murders must be extremely heinous or carried out with cold, deliberate intent. For a defendant to be executed, at least one of these conditions must be proven beyond a reasonable doubt.

Prosecutors tried to persuade the jury during the three-month sentence hearing that aggravating factors were present in this case.

"It was planned. It served a purpose. Additionally, it was a planned massacre" Michael Satz, the main prosecutor, said during his final remarks.
He continued, "The defendant had a plan, he talked about it, and he carried it out.

However, the three jurors who voted against the death punishment did so because of mitigating factors that the defense had persistently raised. These, they found, exceeded the aggravating circumstances put forth by the prosecution.

The gunman's mother's heavy drinking and smoking during his pregnancy caused him to have fetal alcohol spectrum disorder, which the defense attorneys argued was what motivated his violent behavior. This was the most important mitigating factor, and it was extensively discussed by the defense attorneys during the trial.

Melisa McNeill, the principal defense attorney, said in court: "In the womb, he was condemned. Do we kill brain-damaged, mentally ill, and broken people in a civilized society?"

In the latter phases of the trial, when it started to dominate the proceedings, Mr. Satz disputed this. He asserted that "whether or not his mother smoked when she was pregnant did not convert [him] into a mass murderer."

But in the end, the jury was unable to agree unanimously on the death punishment despite weighing horrifying evidence and debating for seven hours.

"That is how the jury process operates. Some of the jurors simply believed that penalty to be the proper one "The jury foreman, Mr. Thomas, stated. "It is a moral choice. Everyone is entitled to an opinion."

<u>families devastated as the shooter gets away with his life.</u>

The murderer of 17 people at Parkland, Florida's Marjory Stoneman Douglas High School was not given the death penalty. For the shooting on February 14, 2018, a jury recommended that the defendant, 24, should serve his entire life in prison. As the verdict was read out in court, relatives of the victims were upset and furious.

On November 1, a sentencing hearing will take place.

In October of last year, Nikolas Cruz, the shooter, entered a plea of guilty to the killings. It was the most deadly mass shooting case that a jury has ever heard in the US.

Those who lost loved ones denounced the decision to spare him from the death penalty as "unreal" and "wrong" at a press conference that followed.

The father of one of the victims, Jaime Guttenberg, 14, stated, "I could not be more disappointed in what occurred today."
"I'm in awe. I'm heartbroken, "he said. "There are 17 victims who are still waiting for justice. Today, this jury let our families down."

The jury's verdict was a setback for the prosecution, who had consistently argued that the acts were "cold, planned, and premeditated," and that they matched Florida's criteria for "aggravating elements" that call for the death penalty.

A death sentence would have required a unanimous decision.

While the jury agreed that there were circumstances that would support the death penalty, it became clear as each of the 17 counts was read out in court that at least one juror also thought there were "mitigating circumstances" that supported life in prison.

The features of many of the family members present in court showed distress. Tony Montalto shook his head repeatedly. Gina, his daughter, was killed in the attack. As the count about Gina was given out, his wife Jennifer, who was in his arms, rested her head on his shoulder.

A few other family members were crying softly. As soon as he heard the jury's recommendation for a life sentence rather than the death penalty, Corey Hixon—whose father Christopher Hixon perished in the attack—rose and fled the room.

Ilan Alhadeff, whose daughter Alyssa was killed, told reporters after the court that the gunman was "not a human being - he's an animal."
"I pray that the animal endures pain in prison everyday", he prayed. "And that his life is brief."

The public lawyer for Broward County in charge of the defense team, Gordon Weekes, urged the general public to "respect the process" that resulted in the verdict.

A solemn opportunity to consider the community's need for healing, he continued, is presented by the decision, in his opinion.

The governors of Florida, Ron DeSantis, a Republican, and Charlie Crist, a Democrat, both declared that they thought the gunman ought to have been executed.

In this case, Mr. DeSantis stated, "I just don't think anything else is appropriate but a capital sentence."

The shooter entered Marjory Stoneman Douglas High School at the age of 19 and started firing with an AR-15 rifle that he had lawfully purchased. A total of 34 persons had been shot within four minutes. Seventeen of them were slain, including three staff members and 14 pupils.

The incident continues to rank among the bloodiest school shootings in American history.

The shooter remained in the vicinity after purchasing a soft drink at a local fast-food restaurant, managing to flee the scene of the crime by disguising himself as a student. Police quickly detained him near the school, at a distance of around two miles (3.2 km).

Prosecutors revealed evidence that the attack had been planned following the killings. The shooter looked up previous mass murders and declared online that he would show "no compassion." The shooter declared in one video, shot days before the incident, that he intended to become the year's "next school shooter" and that his objective was to kill at least 20 people.

The gunman's attorneys tried to paint him as mentally sick, a young man whose mind had been "poisoned" by his mother's drinking and drug usage during his terrible childhood.
The shooting sparked a new round of gun debate in the US and sparked a wave of student action.

Cameron Kasky, David Hogg, X Gonzalez, and Sarah Chadwick were among the survivors who made social media appeals for tougher gun control regulations and the ability to attend school without fear of being shot in the days following the tragedy. The group continues to advocate for legislative goals like tighter regulation of firearms and holding the gun lobby "accountable." However, its legislative objectives, such as a prohibition on assault rifles and large-capacity magazines, have been difficult to achieve.